IMAGES
of America

CALIFORNIA'S
CITRUS HERITAGE

D1602672

Orange towers, like this impressive display made with fruits from Pasadena for the State Citrus Fair of 1891, appeared frequently at produce shows. These exhibitions laid the groundwork for comprehensive permanent shows in later decades, like the National Orange Show, which began in San Bernardino in 1911. (A.K. Smiley Public Library.)

ON THE COVER: While packinghouses relied on machinery to prepare oranges and lemons for transit, fieldworkers completed their labor by hand. Citrus workers packed oranges into field boxes to bring to packinghouses, like this grove operated by the Redlands Orange Growers Association in 1901. (A.K. Smiley Public Library.)

IMAGES
of America

CALIFORNIA'S
CITRUS HERITAGE

Benjamin T. Jenkins

ARCADIA
PUBLISHING

Copyright © 2021 by Benjamin T. Jenkins
ISBN 978-1-4671-0767-9

Published by Arcadia Publishing
Charleston, South Carolina

Printed in the United States of America

Library of Congress Control Number: 2021947732

For all general information, please contact Arcadia Publishing:
Telephone 843-853-2070
Fax 843-853-0044
E-mail sales@arcadiapublishing.com
For customer service and orders:
Toll-Free 1-888-313-2665

Visit us on the Internet at www.arcadiapublishing.com

*To Margo, for all the love you've given and all
the wonderful years yet to come*

CONTENTS

ACKNOWLEDGMENTS

This project would have been impossible without generous support from many talented archivists, librarians, and historians across California.

At the A.K. Smiley Public Library, in Redlands, Nathan Gonzales helped me find wonderful historical images, as did Allan Lagumbay at the Pomona Public Library. I thank Henry Golas for his permission to use "Frasher Fotos"—taken by photographer Burton Frasher—that I found at the Pomona Public Library.

At the Special Collections of the University of Southern California Libraries, I am grateful to Claude Zachary, Yuriy Scherbina, and Wayne Shoaf for their help.

Jennifer Marlatt at the Corona Public Library and Karen Raines at the Rivera Library, University of California, Riverside, were quite helpful. I also thank Amanda Lanthorne at San Diego State University and Jordan Smith of Postcard America. Robyn G. Peterson and Katie Grim at the Museum of Riverside similarly rendered excellent reference service.

At the Honnold Mudd Library of the Claremont Colleges, Ashley Larson and Ayat Agah provided excellent research support. At the Special Collections of the Young Research Library at University of California, Los Angeles (UCLA), I thank Molly Haigh and Simon Elliot. My thanks also to Paul Farnham for permission to use some of the images from the collections at UCLA.

Richard H. Barker and Tom Pulley, longtime California citrus historians, provided images for this work.

At Arcadia Publishing, I thank Erin Vosgien for approaching me about this project and Stacia Bannerman for her editorial expertise and production prowess.

My family has supported my long-running fascination with the citrus industry. Mom and Dad instilled a lifelong interest in community learning, for which I thank them. Margo, my beloved wife, provided a second set of eyes for the project and put up with my relentless talks about citrus. The greatest thanks go to her.

INTRODUCTION

From approximately 1870 to 1950, an immensely profitable orange empire dominated Southern California. From Pasadena to Redlands and Riverside and Santa Barbara to San Diego, orange and lemon groves dominated the landscape. For decades, citrus fruits were synonymous with the area.

It took centuries for this commercial ascendance to solidify. Citrus fruits originated in southeast Asia but did not arrive in North America until the Europeans arrived in the so-called New World. The citrus industry came to California in the early 19th century. Around 1803, Spanish missionaries brought the first oranges to Mission San Gabriel in the southern portion of the province they called Alta California. Spanish priests, soldiers, and settlers forced Indigenous peoples to practice agriculture in the fields surrounding the missions, including tending the orange trees at Mission San Gabriel.

For most of the Spanish and Mexican periods of California history, cattle-ranching and the hide-and-tallow trade eclipsed oranges, which remained a luxury crop. Southern California remained rural and isolated during the gold rush of the 1840s and 1850s. When the first transcontinental railroad came to the Golden State, it terminated in the San Francisco Bay area, avoiding Southern California.

By the 1860s, droughts and cattle die-offs led to opportunities for newly settled Americans in Southern California. As railroads finally reached that corner of the state in the 1870s, settlers from the eastern United States grew new varieties of oranges. The Washington navel orange, introduced to Riverside around 1873, became lucratively successful by the end of the 19th century. Widely considered tastier than other varieties of oranges, the Washington navel won high honors at local and regional citrus fairs. By the 1890s, they had earned international recognition, and customers across the United States sought oranges grown in California.

A cornucopia of citrus fruits joined Washington navel oranges in the groves of California. The Valencia orange thrived in the groves of Orange County, which was carved out of territory formerly belonging to Los Angeles County in 1889. Lemon growers cultivated Eureka and Lisbon varieties of that fruit along the coast, particularly near Santa Barbara and Ventura. At its height, the orange (and lemon) empire stretched across huge swaths of California, particularly the southern part of California. Even distant outposts like Imperial Valley, located in the arid southeastern corner of the state, adopted citrus agriculture in the form of grapefruit.

The citrus industry solidified American control of Southern California, just as the gold rush did for other parts of the state. Oranges and lemons brought California into to the commercial orbit of the United States.

Other important elements, namely scientific development, water, and the growth of an industrial infrastructure, facilitated the rise of the citrus empire. The arrival of railroads in Southern California aided the commercial possibilities of citrus agriculture. By 1876, the Southern Pacific Railroad, soon to become a transcontinental route linking California to New Orleans, reached Los Angeles. Within a decade, the Atchison, Topeka & Santa Fe Railroad laid tracks to towns including San Bernardino and National City, key orange-growing centers that became major rail hubs for this transcontinental line. The Santa Fe and Southern Pacific Railroads laid tracks across the orange empire in the 1880s and 1890s. They engaged in rate wars that, at one point, reduced travel fare from the Midwest to California to $1. More importantly, railroads transported oranges and lemons to markets across the United States.

Unlike agriculturalists in other parts of the country, orange and lemon growers did not perceive themselves as farmers but as agribusinessmen. To better combat high railroad raids and curtail the financial influence of middlemen in eastern markets, in 1893, citrus growers across California banded together to form the California Fruit Growers Exchange (CFGE) to collectively control production of citrus across the Golden State. By the 20th century, CFGE controlled most orange and lemon production in California. CFGE's successful advertising of its Sunkist brand made it ubiquitous wherever fruits were sold across America. Similarly, although the group was not as successful as Sunkist, the Mutual Orange Distributors, which started in Redlands in the early 20th century, achieved control over a sizeable minority of California citrus production.

The citrus industry had a major economic impact on California. It linked Californians from all social backgrounds and economic classes across the financial spectrum. Rich white growers owned most citrus groves. They cooperated with the state government and scientists from the University of California to bring the latest botanical, entomological, and irrigational techniques to bear on their industry. Asian Americans, Mexican Americans, and Indigenous peoples worked in orange and lemon fields and packinghouses across California. Women also participated in the citrus industry. Some affluent women owned and operated groves; however, it was more common to see women working in packinghouses. This diversity gave all segments of California's society a stake in the citrus industry.

Workers, especially people of color, built communities for themselves within the citrus industry. For instance, during the Great Depression, Mexican Americans created the Confederación de Uniones Obreros Mexicanos, a labor union that pushed for higher wages in the citrus industry. Community in citrus country thus formed from the bottom up. However, failed strikes in the 1930s led to the demise of the union, demonstrating the limits of workers' efforts to improve their lives in the citrus industry.

Citrus growers manipulated the California landscape to meet their needs. The cultivation of oranges and lemons was not a totally rural enterprise, which distinguished it from existing farming models used in other parts of the United States. Instead, Californians who generated wealth through citrus fruits reinvested their profits in their communities. Money from the citrus industry allowed Californians to develop electrified packinghouses that used state-of-the-art technology. Landowners built lavish homes in affluent neighborhoods as status symbols.

The orange empire overcame severe environmental limitations. Growers built intricate water systems to fight the natural aridity of Southern California. They designed orchard heaters to prevent frosts from killing orange and lemon trees and developed scientific methods of pest control. The Citrus Experiment Station, an outgrowth of the University of California that opened in Riverside in 1907, spearheaded many of these scientific developments.

The citrus industry transformed over the latter part of the 20th century but retained a powerful commercial influence on California. Following the end of World War II in 1945 and the rise of heavy industry in Southern California, citrus growers shifted north to the state's Central Valley, where orange-growing became more profitable than ever.

Sunkist remains an important link to California's citrus heritage. The company, which reached the century mark in 1993, continues to market products from the Golden State across the country and remains synonymous with quality citrus. Scientific research and crop management also continue to thrive in 21st-century California. The Citrus Research Board and its *Citrograph* magazine offer up-to-date information on scientific developments, including strategies for minimizing pests and making efficient use of California's limited water supply. The periodical's name hearkens back to the *California Citrograph*, published by members of the citrus industry in the early- to mid-20th century, further demonstrating the Golden State's unbroken connection to oranges and lemons.

One

Padres, Fur Trappers, and Yankee Transplants

California's citrus heritage began in the early 19th century. Franciscan missionaries (*padres*, as Catholic priests were known in Spanish) and Spanish settlers brought fruit seeds to Alta California when establishing religious missions in the region in 1769. Under the direction of the padres, Indigenous Californians planted the first orange grove at Mission San Gabriel in 1803 or 1804. Indigenous laborers at the missions were forced to work the land and care for the trees, turning this into the first citrus orchard in California. At its height, Mission San Gabriel had 400 sweet orange trees spread across six acres. This orchard fell into decline by 1834, when the mission system of California was secularized.

During the Californio period, when the region was nominally part of the Mexican Republic (from 1821 to 1846), foreign settlers around Los Angeles planted oranges on a larger scale. Most notable among these were Jean-Louis Vignes, a French settler, and William Wolfskill, a fur trapper from Kentucky. Vignes's planting, located close to the small town of Los Angeles, consisted of 25 orange trees, which he took from Mission San Gabriel. Wolfskill, Vignes's neighbor, noted the success of these trees, and planted his own grove in 1841 using fruits from the mission. At 70 acres, Wolfskill's grove was the largest in North America at the time and became commercially successful. After Wolfskill's death in 1866, his son Joseph took control of the grove. Eleven years later, Joseph Wolfskill sent the first oranges from California by rail, shipping them to St. Louis and generating press for citrus fruits grown in the Golden State.

The success of Wolfskill's orange grove spurred a generation of émigré American settlers from the northeastern United States (Yankees), and by the 1870s, an orange empire emanating from the settlement of Riverside encompassed a wide swath of California. In 1871, L.C. Waite brought the first oranges to Riverside. From 1868 to 1875, Thomas Garey, a botanist in Los Angeles, imported many new kinds of oranges to the Golden State. However, it was not until the arrival of the Washington navel orange that the industry achieved its greatest success.

Citrus agriculture began in 1804, when Franciscan missionaries brought the first orange trees to Mission San Gabriel. The mission, shown here in approximately 1890, was maintained by Indigenous peoples like the Tongvas, who lived in San Gabriel Valley before Europeans arrived. Spanish missionaries never practiced citriculture on a large scale. (Huntington Library.)

Citrus trees originated in Asia and were not native to California. In addition to being artificially introduced by European and American colonizers, orange and lemon trees were frequently manufactured through advanced botanical practices, including grafting. A young citrus tree, like the one pictured at right around 1910, would have the branch of the desired fruit grafted onto it. When it matured, the adult tree would grow the fruits of those from the grafted bud. The same basic system remained in place for years, with a tree in La Verne (pictured below) undergoing the same budding process in 1930. (Both, University of Southern California Libraries and California Historical Society.)

Orange trees usually came into bearing five to seven years after being planted. In this image from approximately 1900, two men inspect young orange trees, possibly nursery stock, long before the specimens could produce fruit. The lengthy maturation of citrus trees required those who owned groves to depend on other sources of income and restricted participation in the industry to wealthier members of society. (A.K. Smiley Public Library.)

Citrus agriculture had deep roots in San Bernardino, located 50 miles east of Los Angeles. Carleton Watkins preserved this c. 1878 photograph of the Van Leuven grove. Anson Van Leuven was one of the earliest pioneers of orange-growing in inland Southern California. (Huntington Library.)

William Wolfskill (pictured) was a pivotal figure in the early California citrus industry. A trapper from Kentucky, Wolfskill settled in Los Angeles when the city was part of Mexican California. In 1841, he acquired trees from nearby Mission San Gabriel, which served as the foundation for one of the most successful citrus orchards in North America. (Citrus Roots Collection.)

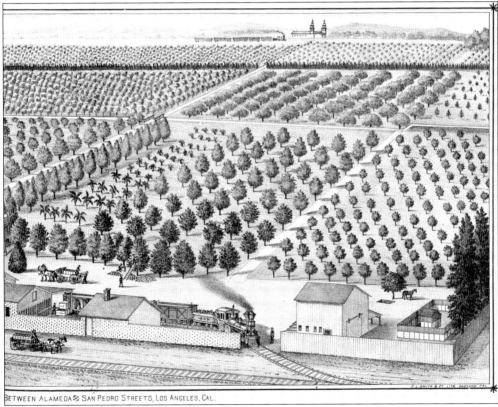

BETWEEN ALAMEDA & SAN PEDRO STREETS, LOS ANGELES, CAL.

After William Wolfskill's death in 1866, his son Joseph took control of the grove, which appears in this image from 1880. Joseph Wolfskill was the first Californian to ship oranges by rail. He even convinced the Southern Pacific Railroad to open a depot on his property. (Wilson Library, University of La Verne.)

Scenic vistas of citrus groves appeared in countless photographs, postcards, and promotional materials designed to entice travelers to visit California. In this view of the area around Highland from 1915, a passenger train steams through the groves. Pruned trees appear in the foreground. Fieldworkers coated the trunks in white lime to protect the trees from being harmed by the sun. (Citrus Roots Collection.)

Orange trees took years before they came into bearing. Typically, it required 5 to 7 years for a tree to mature and produce fruit, as was the case for the 10-year-old specimen photographed about 1910 and shown at right. Citrus growers had to find other sources of income until their trees matured. As a result, only wealthy residents, primarily those who had arrived from New England, planted orange and lemon trees en masse. The below image shows an orange or lemon tree on the property of H.S. Snow in Riverside around the same time. (Both, University of Southern California Libraries and California Historical Society.)

Citrus trees required more attention than crops like the grains that dominated midwestern agriculture. Protecting them from pests and diseases and making sure that they grew properly required constant care. Workers enveloped young trees, like those in this 1912 image, with yucca wraps. (A.K. Smiley Public Library.)

An avenue of orange trees along Sunny Slope in San Gabriel made for an eye-catching image. This photograph was taken by famed western photographer Carleton E. Watkins around 1880. L.J. Rose, best known for his role in the early wine industry of California, owned this property. (Huntington Library.)

This c. 1883 image of Pasadena speaks to the idyllic character of the early town. The San Gabriel Mountains in the far background dwarf the modest buildings and citrus groves. Selling fruits produced by these trees would eventually allow Pasadenans to pave streets and build homes, banks, and other structures. In short, returns on citrus investments enhanced the communities of California. (Huntington Library.)

While the profits of citrus agriculture facilitated urban development in the 20th century, early orange- and lemon-growing communities were sparse. This image of Pasadena, which would become famous for lavish homes on the Millionaire's Row of Orange Grove Boulevard, attests to the humble beginnings of the city in the 1870s. (Huntington Library.)

Carleton E. Watkins produced this c. 1878 image of the ranch belonging to General George Stoneman in San Gabriel. The photograph provides an excellent view of an early citrus grove. To visitors like Watkins, the land seemed desolate but for the endless expanses of fruit trees. (Huntington Library.)

Although the capitalists and advertisers of the citrus belt portrayed mature groves as a natural part of the California landscape, orange and lemon trees were not native to the region. Groves such as this one pictured in Redlands around 1910 represented human additions to the region. (A.K. Smiley Public Library.)

Recalling the *zanjas* (ditches) of Spanish California, the early citrus industry watered groves with simple dirt channels. The man who appears in the image at right alongside a ditch in Redlands may have been cleaning the channel. This was a critical task, since orange and lemon trees require constant supplies of water—a rare and valuable resource in Southern California, where most of the early citrus groves appeared. The woman in the below image was likely a visitor or potentially the owner of a grove. Women who participated in the citrus industry typically worked in packinghouses, not fields. (Both, A.K. Smiley Public Library.)

18723—Irrigating Endless Avenues of Orange Trees, Redlands, Calif.

An early fruit-drying yard appears in this undated image. This photograph was taken at a site once known as North Ontario Colony. Citizens later renamed the town Upland to differentiate their home from its older neighbor to the south, the Ontario colony settled by George Chaffey. (Pomona Public Library.)

Citrus trees thrive in semitropical environments like Southern California. However, they are vulnerable to frost, which occurred periodically in the early 20th century in California, threatening the profitability of the citrus industry. This image, taken from a professional study published in 1919, shows a Valencia orange tree devastated by cold. (Citrus Roots Collection.)

While the cultivation of citrus fruits eventually differed from previous forms of agriculture through mechanization and scientific management, early groves relied on traditional technologies and domestic animals. Horses, for instance, hauled crops and prepared the land for planting, as shown in this image of an early orange grove. (A.K. Smiley Public Library.)

Horses, like the ones pictured here in Redlands in 1912, hauled boxes of oranges and lemons from the fields to packinghouses. Automobiles, especially trucks, replaced animal labor in the groves of California's citrus industry in subsequent decades. Also notable in this image are the power lines in the background. (A.K. Smiley Public Library.)

Old and new agricultural methods and technologies overlapped as citrus workers hauled fruits from fields to packinghouses. While the horse-drawn wagon shown here laden with fruit had yet to be displaced by automobile transit, the utility pole and electrical wires in the background attest to the mechanization of the packinghouse. (A.K. Smiley Public Library.)

Two

THE ORANGE EMPIRE

When Eliza Tibbets came to Riverside, California, in the 1870s, she did not realize she carried with her the seeds of a commercial empire. Tibbets had received two or three Bahia navel orange trees from the US Department of Agriculture. They produced delicious, seedless fruits. Since Riverside had no canals in the 1870s, Tibbets used dirty dishwater to nourish her trees.

The results of Tibbets's work were spectacular and far-reaching. By 1879, fruits from Tibbets's navel orange trees were winning awards at an agricultural fair in Riverside. The fruits were eventually called Washington navel oranges to give them a distinctly American name. Tibbets's neighbors clamored for fruits from her Washington navel orange trees to graft onto their own specimens. Before long, residents from Riverside and other towns across Southern California joined them. Washington navel orange trees bore fruit and become commercially profitable by the 1880s, leading to a plethora of towns to emulate Riverside. Observers agreed that citrus trees thrived in California's sunny climate.

After the success of Tibbets's fruits, the orange empire of Southern California rapidly expanded. Beginning in rural towns like Riverside, Redlands, Pasadena, and Anaheim, the empire eventually encompassed large sections of Los Angeles, San Bernardino, Santa Barbara, and San Diego Counties. New counties, such as Orange and Riverside, came into being thanks to the returns on investment from oranges.

From Pasadena to Riverside, the Washington navel dominated agriculture. In Orange County, the Valencia orange became the most sought-after crop. Out of Fullerton, the major citriculturist Charles Chapman led growers across Orange County to adopt the Valencia. Although Valencia oranges took longer to ripen, they did so in the spring, offering an alternative to the Washington navels, which were harvested in winter. The orange empire could seemingly offer fruit year-round.

Lemons eventually joined oranges in the citrus groves of Southern California. Near the coast, in Santa Barbara and the new Ventura County, the Eureka and Lisbon lemons thrived. At Limoneira Ranch in Santa Paula, lemon magnate Charles C. Teague established an expansive grove and became one of the leading figures of the citrus industry. Goleta in Santa Barbara County similarly became a major center of lemon production.

Across Southern California, the planting of citrus groves dictated urban growth. The locations of orange and lemon trees and packinghouses influenced the construction of railroads, banks, schools—indeed, entire communities. By 1900, the orange empire had become a dominant commercial and cultural force in California.

Eliza Tibbets, shown here around 1880, brought the first navel orange trees to Riverside in the 1870s. She provided cuttings from the specimens to her neighbors, who planted their own Washington navel orange trees. Local legend maintains that, when necessary, she used dirty dishwater to nourish her trees. (UC Riverside.)

One of the first Washington navel orange trees was planted at Riverside, California, by Eliza Tibbets around 1873. These trees were replanted numerous times over the years and received grafts and underwent other procedures to overcome infection. One of these parent navel orange trees still stands in Riverside. (Museum of Riverside.)

Pictures like this c. 1890 panoramic vista of Riverside demonstrated the all-encompassing nature of citrus in Southern California. Communities planted orange and lemon trees across the landscape. Through such large-scale plantings, the industry became the backbone of agriculture in Southern California by the 1890s. (University of Southern California Libraries and California Historical Society.)

Washington navel oranges accounted for the most acreage of inland Southern California's citrus belt, but owners sometimes intercropped other varieties into their groves. Louisa Vezzetti of Riverside, whose property in Redlands appears in this image, planted lemon trees (shown in the foreground) to complement her Washington navels. (A.K. Smiley Public Library.)

The profitability of the citrus industry led to the improvement of communities across California and the creation of a modern infrastructure. Broad thoroughfares imposed order on rapidly developing landscapes. Citrus growers separated themselves from their neighbors, including the pickers and packers who served them. In Riverside, wealthy citrus-grove owners created the Arlington neighborhood, serviced by the impressive Magnolia Avenue. It appears, lined with palm trees, in the above image. As with many geographical features of California, it also became the template for a citrus crate label shown below. (Above, the Huntington Library; below, Citrus Roots Collection.)

Pasadena, one of the earliest major citrus towns in Southern California, opulently celebrated returns on early orange investments. Many orange growers lived on Orange Grove Boulevard, the lavish avenue shown on this postcard. Nicknamed Millionaire's Row, this section of Pasadena was home to many architecturally significant homes. Many original homes from the city's early history are still standing along the boulevard. (Postcard America.)

While railroads shipped most of the oranges and lemons exported from California, they could not account for overseas travel. Workers also loaded the citrus bounty of the Golden State onto boats for international shipment, as shown in this 1928 image. Oranges from California even reached the court of Great Britain's Queen Victoria. (Pomona Public Library.)

Early citrus fairs, like the one held at Riverside in 1885 (above), seem primitive when compared to later, more comprehensive efforts. The below image commemorates the first citrus fair in Pasadena, which played a pivotal role in the development of the citrus industry. Although quaint by later standards, these fairs played an important part in bringing together citrus growers from across Southern California who shared information about planting, irrigating, and marketing crops. The networks formed at these events laid the groundwork for the cooperative associations that later controlled the citrus industry. (Above, UC Riverside; below, Pasadena Public Library.)

By the end of the 19th century, Orange County had earned its name. Originally part of Los Angeles County, Orange broke away to achieve independence in 1889. The Valencia orange ruled the groves here, including those of Irvine Ranch. By the early 20th century, the owners of the Irvine Ranch were the largest landowners in Orange County, with 600 acres dedicated to citrus agriculture. (Citrus Roots Collection.)

Lemons thrived in Orange County, which is closer to the coast than Riverside or San Bernardino and thus more beneficial for that strain of citrus. This image shows Tustin, California, in the early 20th century. The text on the photograph refers to Lemon Heights, reflecting the tendency among citrus growers to stress their geographic elevation, as with Redlands's Smiley Heights or Riverside's Arlington Heights. (Citrus Roots Collection.)

Many ranches in the citrus belt laid claim to the title of largest citrus grove over the years. Bastanchury Ranch in Fullerton, shown here, identified itself as such in the early 20th century. The first appearance of Valencia oranges in Orange County occurred in the city of Fullerton in 1875. (Tom Pulley.)

Citrus groves coexisted with other important segments of California's economy in the early 20th century. For example, developers often sunk oil wells in or around orange groves, like the ones pictured here in the Atwood district of Placentia in Orange County in 1932. (University of Southern California Libraries and California Historical Society.)

Before planting orange or lemon trees, growers had to modify the landscape of Southern California. Pioneers like George Chaffey experimented with creative forms of development. Chaffey, who came to California from Canada, started the communities of Etiwanda and Ontario. He inaugurated a system in which members of the community received shares in the distribution of water—a critical ingredient for agriculture in semiarid Southern California. In Ontario, George Chaffey designed Euclid Avenue as the central thoroughfare for his colony. Trees dotted this stately route, which ran from the tracks of the Southern Pacific Railroad to the San Gabriel Mountains. Streets like Euclid Avenue, pictured here in the 1880s, brought geographic order to the landscape of the citrus belt. (Citrus Roots Collection.)

The city of Santa Paula in Ventura County was the heart of lemon production in Southern California. This image of a lemon packinghouse from the early 20th century gives some indication of the size of the citrus industry in Santa Paula. The citrus industry was a leading employer in communities across California, as shown by the impressive workforce pictured outside this packinghouse. (Citrus Roots Collection.)

Few men shaped the citrus industry of California as extensively as Charles Collins Teague. As the operator of Limoneira, Teague oversaw 900 acres of citrus. Teague promoted the use of orchard heating, and for years led the California Fruit Growers Exchange as its president. During World War II, Teague advocated for the use of Mexican labor in California's agricultural sector in the form of the Bracero Program. (Citrus Roots Collection.)

Advertisers enjoyed showing citrus fruits lined up against scenic backdrops like waves of the Pacific Ocean lapping against San Diego. By 1900, citrus had gained a significant foothold in San Diego County. Appropriately, citrus trees lined Orange Avenue leading to the Hotel del Coronado, one of the best-known historic resorts in the San Diego area. (UC San Diego.)

GRAPEFRUIT GROWING IN IMPERIAL VALLEY.   EL CENTRO, CALIFORNIA.

Imperial Valley is located in arid southeastern California. It became an agricultural center by the early 20th century thanks to massive water projects that drew from the Colorado River for irrigation. Citrus fruits thrived here alongside other crops, including carrots and peas. Grapefruits—like the ones in this image—grew plentifully. (San Diego State University.)

While Southern Californians claimed that oranges and lemons could only thrive in their corner of the state, counties outside that area also took part in citrus agriculture. Porterville, in Tulare County (pictured), boasted many productive orange groves of its own, solidifying the city's commercial reputation. (Claremont Colleges Libraries Special Collections.)

Aerial photographs like this one captured the expansive nature of citrus fields. Such pictures were often taken from balloons. The geographic order of the neatly lined rows of trees, roads, and ditches, even before paved streets and canals became common, testifies to the extensive infrastructure found in citrus groves. (A.K. Smiley Public Library.)

Gardens like Smiley Heights in Redlands worked to attract tourists to the scenic beauty of the citrus belt. This c.1900 image draws attention to the paved path running through the park, which was ideal for tourists in horse-drawn carriages and, later, automobiles. (A.K. Smiley Public Library.)

The mountains of Southern California, which were important geographic markers for Indigenous peoples, Spanish missionaries, and Mexican ranchers, also became crucial to citrus growers. In addition to shielding the southland from storms originating in the Pacific Ocean, they gathered rainwater. The San Bernardino Mountains (pictured) were the source of the Santa Ana River that served the groves of Riverside and Orange County. (A.K. Smiley Public Library.)

Mt. San Bernardino from Smiley Heights.

Smiley Heights exemplified citriculturists' belief that the human touch was a positive force that could improve the landscape of California. The lake, trees, and flowers (shown here in full bloom around 1900) demanded a hand-colored image, which Redlands circulated to promote civic pride. (A.K. Smiley Public Library.)

Lake in Smiley Heights.

35

Money from the sale of citrus fruits allowed towns in Southern California to invest in community improvement. Tapping into the City Beautiful movement of the late 19th century, Alfred and Albert Smiley, civic leaders in Redlands, created Canyon Crest Park, which residents dubbed Smiley Heights. The park appears in this c. 1905 image complete with lush flowers and trees. (A.K. Smiley Public Library.)

Panoramas of Southern California's San Gabriel and San Bernardino Valleys dominated promotional imagery related to citrus. Photographs like this one of Redlands around 1900 juxtaposed orange groves against mountains and valleys. The use of oranges to frame the picture suggests the centrality of citrus agriculture in making such remarkable vistas possible. (A.K. Smiley Public Library.)

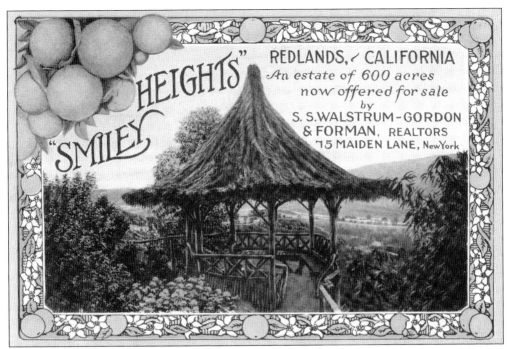

"SMILEY HEIGHTS"

REDLANDS, CALIFORNIA

An estate of 600 acres now offered for sale
by
S. S. WALSTRUM-GORDON
& FORMAN, REALTORS
15 MAIDEN LANE, NewYork

While images of the citrus belt were partly designed to lure tourists, advertisers also used them to encourage permanent settlement. This promotional photograph for Smiley Heights in Redlands demonstrates how promoters used the landscape to attract people from outside the Golden State. Many early grove owners in California came from the northeastern United States, particularly New England. (A.K. Smiley Public Library.)

The delicate nature of citrus trees and their fruits required workers to use primitive technologies for planting and harvesting. The worker shown here is using horses to pull a spike-tooth harrow in 1912, perhaps to prepare for the planting of additional trees. (A.K. Smiley Public Library.)

Cultivating Old Orang Grove with Spike-Tooth Harrow
april 16, 1912

In addition to shipping oranges and lemons, railroads in Southern California relied on citrus for tourism. Excursion trains from Los Angeles took travelers through the groves of the San Gabriel and San Bernardino Valleys as far east as Redlands, then south to Riverside. Railroads helped local communities sell land to potential residents for the purpose of growing citrus, which benefitted emerging cities and guaranteed future revenue for the railways in the form of freight charges. Riverside appears above with a Southern Pacific Railroad train chugging through the groves. The 1880s image below may depict either San Dimas or Redlands. (Both, University of Southern California Libraries and California Historical Society.)

Railroads played a pivotal role in the development of the citrus industry in California. The Santa Fe Railroad provided refrigerator and ventilated cars to preserve fruit in transit. In the 1880s, this railroad played a key role in breaking up the monopoly the Southern Pacific Railroad had on transportation in Southern California by opening lines to crucial orange- and lemon-growing settlements like National City and San Bernardino. (Pomona Public Library.)

The Union Pacific and Southern Pacific Railroads provided a tremendous service to the citrus industry when they jointly created the Pacific Fruit Express (PFE). Through the PFE, shippers had access to a fleet of refrigerator railcars, like those shown here in Los Angeles in 1932. Black-and-white photography could not capture the distinctive yellow paint of the PFE cars. (University of Southern California Libraries and California Historical Society.)

Promoters of the citrus industry sought national recognition for their accomplishments. One highlight occurred in 1903, when Pres. Theodore Roosevelt visited the Mission Inn in Riverside to replant one of the parent navel orange trees that made the city famous. Roosevelt is pictured holding a shovel at the event. (University of Southern California Libraries and California Historical Society.)

Members of California's citrus industry wanted to preserve their history. They wrote books and installed memorials designed to glorify their roles in California's agricultural revolution. Citizens in Riverside preserved one of the surviving parent Washington navel orange trees brought to the city by Eliza Tibbets. It is pictured here in 1932 at the Mission Inn. (Adelbert Bartlett papers [Collection 1300]. Library Special Collections, Charles E. Young Research Library, UCLA.)

Three

GROVES AND FIELDWORKERS

While wealthy men and women owned groves, laborers completed the work necessary to maintain the citrus empire. Work in the California citrus industry broadly fit into two domains: fieldwork in the groves and packing work in packinghouses. Laborers from a variety of backgrounds worked in both areas.

Fieldwork in the California citrus industry was physically challenging. Workers slowly and carefully removed fruits from trees by hand to avoid bruising them. Overseers prevented workers from speaking during the workday, and laborers often toiled so hard that they developed arthritis. They climbed ladders, scratched their hands as they picked fruit, fumigated crops, dug irrigation ditches, and lit orchard heaters on freezing nights. Such ardor brought delicious oranges and lemons from California to kitchens and parlors across the United States.

As early as the mission era, Indigenous peoples formed a crucial segment of the laboring population, as they were forced to tend to the oranges introduced at Mission San Gabriel. By the mid-19th century, when orange trees started to spread across Southern California, Indigenous Californians still accounted for a sizable portion of the state's agricultural labor force.

Settlers from East Asia joined Indigenous workers in the orange groves. Chinese immigrants came to California in search of gold during the 1850s. Subsequently, they became central to the railroad industry as tracks were laid across the American West. By 1885, many Chinese immigrants had become farmworkers, and according to one estimate from that year, they accounted for as much as 80 percent of the farmhands in the citrus industry. Later, Filipinos and Japanese Americans joined them in the citrus groves.

Multiple factors brought Mexicans and Mexican Americans into the California citrus industry. The chaos of the Mexican Revolution made even low-wage jobs in California attractive. By 1920, Mexicans eclipsed Asians as the largest population of farmworkers. In the 1930s, forced repatriation programs resulted in the deportation of Mexican and Mexican American workers. However, the Bracero Program of 1942, launched by the US and Mexican governments to fill vacancies in the farm industry during World War II, brought Mexican fieldworkers back to California's orange and lemon groves.

By 1900, Riverside was blanketed with Washington navel orange groves. Its financial success convinced people in nearby towns to plant citrus ranches of their own. These images of groves in the affluent town of Redlands were taken around 1901. The photographs show the three-legged ladders that pickers used to ascend the trees to remove fruits by hand. Mechanically harvesting citrus crops was impossible, as lemons and oranges can bruise or cut easily, resulting in an opening for infections like the dreaded blue mold. Workers had to handle fruits carefully as they were transported from groves to railroad cars. (Both, A.K. Smiley Public Library.)

The women picking oranges with a worker on a ladder on the property of the Redlands Orange Growers Association were likely posing for this photograph rather than actually working as field hands. The well-dressed man on the right side of the image may have owned the property. (A.K. Smiley Public Library.)

While women rarely worked in the groves, a few owned lemon and orange ranches. The men in this image picked fruit for Mrs. E.C. Sterling of Redlands, California, in 1912. Although men owned most of the land in the citrus belt, newspapers often praised the industrious women who entered the industry and profited from it. (A.K. Smiley Public Library.)

Tourists and the owners of citrus ranches frequently visited the groves of Southern California. In this image featuring a Redlands grove in 1903, women and children enjoy a sightseeing excursion. These visitors may have owned the grove or been related to the proprietor. (A.K. Smiley Public Library.)

Workers of the La Verne Orange Growers Association took a break to pose for this photograph. In La Verne, while some Mexican American workers lived in quarters built by citrus cooperatives, others lived south of the railroad tracks in a segregated community. (Pomona Public Library.)

Mexican American workers like these men formed the backbone of the California citrus industry and dominated the groves of San Gabriel Valley, Orange County, and San Bernardino County. The men pictured below worked in the groves of San Dimas. The Bracero Program, which began in 1942, instated temporary worker permits for Mexican nationals to enter the United States, with many of them going to work in the orange and lemon groves of California. Inaugurated as a wartime measure to overcome labor shortages, the Bracero Program outlasted the conflict by nearly 20 years. (Both, Claremont Colleges Libraries Special Collections.)

Picking lemons, as shown here, required simple equipment. Workers wore gloves to protect themselves from thorns and brush, using clippers to safely remove the fruit from the tree. The careful handling of fruits prevented them from becoming bruised or infected and preserved their market value. (University of Southern California Libraries and California Historical Society.)

Southern California Lemon Trees Produce Continuously. Every Month All Fruit Which Is Too Large To Pass Through A Ring Of A Certain Diameter Is Cut Off. Special Clippers Are Used To Avoid Abrasions. Lemons Picked Green Are More Tart Than Lemons Fully Ripe.

This photograph, which shows lemon pickers at the Azusa Foot-Hill Co. Ranch, was colored by hand to suggest the vivacity of the fruit. In reality, lemons typically only appear vibrantly yellow after being washed and processed in a packinghouse. (Pomona Public Library.)

Foot-Hill Co. Ranch, AZUSA, Cal. Picking Lemons.

The political unrest of the Mexican Revolution and a labor shortage during World War I provided push-and-pull factors for Mexican laborers to enter California. This image depicts the multicultural labor force at Chase Ranch American Fruit Growers in Corona. (Corona Public Library.)

Valencia oranges blanketed Orange County. Pickers in Santa Ana, the seat of the county government, are shown in this image around 1900. The attire of the kneeling workers suggests that they may have entered the United States from East Asia. By the 20th century, Filipino and Japanese workers had become indispensable in the lemon and orange fields. (University of Southern California Libraries and California Historical Society.)

The California citrus industry dealt in volume. Fieldworkers packed wagons with as many boxes as their horses could handle, as demonstrated by the vehicles piled high with oranges in this grove in Redlands around 1900. By 1910, Southern Californians shipped 25,000 carloads of oranges and 5,000 carloads of lemons annually, resulting in a return of $20 million to the growers of California. (A.K. Smiley Public Library.)

By 1920, large citrus organizations like the Irvine Valencia Orange Growers Association in Orange County had adopted automobiles. The unusual wheels on the truck in this photograph may indicate that the vehicle was experimental. The palm trees effectively frame the truck, which could carry more field crates than a horse-drawn cart. (Orange Public Library.)

Fruit pickers like those pictured in this camp often lived apart from the rest of their communities. Frequently, their housing was poorer than that of the grove owners for whom they worked. Asian American pickers, for instance, often had little to no access to homeownership. (University of Southern California Libraries and California Historical Society.)

Candid pictures, while uncommon when compared to staged photographs, revealed insights into the work performed in orange and lemon groves. This image was captured near Los Angeles around 1900. Canvas bags, ladders, and field boxes—the three most important items in an orange-picker's toolkit—appear here. (A.K. Smiley Public Library.)

After Congress banned Chinese immigration in the 1880s and California made efforts to curtail Japanese landownership and entry into the Golden State, growers recruited Filipino laborers to work in the citrus industry. Since the United States had acquired the Philippines in 1899 following the Spanish-American War, anti-Asian bias could not prevent Filipinos from voyaging to North America to partake in the citrus industry. (A.K. Smiley Public Library.)

Images of orange pickers, such as these men, obscured the multiracial character of the labor force that drove the citrus industry. Black-and-white photographs often ignored the faces of people of color, particularly the Asian Americans and Indigenous Californians who were so crucial to the early success of the citrus industry. (A.K. Smiley Public Library.)

This picture of an orange grove in inland Southern California juxtaposes the ordered, productive landscape of an orange grove against the rugged and imposing snow-capped mountains in the background. The proximity of sun-bathed orange groves to wintry peaks captivated advertisers, who relied heavily on such imagery. (A.K. Smiley Public Library.)

In 1936, citrus workers in Orange County went on strike for higher wages. Although strikes had occurred before, this work stoppage was the largest that the citrus industry had faced up to that point. Police and private security forces in the groves arrested striking laborers, like the Mexican Americans shown here. (Claremont Colleges Libraries Special Collections.)

Floods required citrus growers and fieldworkers to think creatively. In 1941, the Puddingstone Reservoir near San Dimas flooded nearby groves. Undaunted, workers donned bathing suits and paddled rowboats to the trees to pick fruits. (Los Angeles Times Photographic Archive [Collection 1429]. Library Special Collections, Charles E. Young Research Library, UCLA.)

Four

PACKINGHOUSES

Once workers harvested citrus fruit, they had to prepare it for transport. Initially, they packed fruit in the fields. Over time, this activity was relocated to sheds and, eventually, larger packinghouses. In these buildings, workers washed and dried fruit and graded it, separating pieces of fruit based on the size and quality of the oranges and lemons.

After sorting fruits, workers wrapped them in thin paper and placed them in specially built wooden crates to secure them for transit. Like in the production of other fruit, each packinghouse in the California citrus industry used specialized labels to advertise their products. Workers affixed these to the sides of boxes to build brand loyalty.

Orange and lemon growers typically built packinghouses directly on the tracks of railroads that crisscrossed California. This facilitated the easy transport of goods. To further aid this process, the Southern Pacific and Santa Fe Railroads invested in refrigerator cars and icing stations to prevent oranges and lemons from spoiling during transit from the Golden State.

Early packinghouses relied on human bodies for energy and gas lighting for visibility. By the 20th century, packinghouses had become electrified, allowing packers to operate heavy machinery. Electric motors improved productivity, and electric lights provided superior illumination. New machines filled the packinghouses with a constant mechanical hum as washing machines brushed fruit, conveyors separated fruits based on size, and skilled workers assembled wooden crates by hand.

By 1910, citrus packinghouses had largely standardized layouts that followed the assembly-line model pioneered by automobile manufacturer Henry Ford. The early mechanization of citriculture demonstrated the successful integration of industry with agriculture in the Golden State. Thanks to the modernization of packinghouses, the citrus industry thrived in Southern California through the mid-20th century.

This image shows workers preparing to load orange crates onto a refrigerated railroad car in Ontario, California, around 1920. Many of the crate labels visible in this image come from Upland, a city that was directly next to Ontario. Packers from neighboring towns often pooled resources in shared packinghouses. (University of Southern California Libraries and California Historical Society.)

Early packinghouses were little more than storage sheds, but by the 20th century, they had expanded to accommodate the growth of the citrus industry. This c. 1910 picture of a California Citrus Union packinghouse offers a sense of the massive volume of fruits processed each day. (A.K. Smiley Public Library.)

Prior to 1900, most of the work in California citrus packinghouses—like this one in Riverside—was completed by hand. This included washing and drying oranges and lemons, sorting them by size, and packing them into wooden crates before loading them onto railroad cars. (Museum of Riverside.)

The Covina Citrus Association packinghouse pictured here around 1900 demonstrates the opportunities available to female laborers in orange and lemon production. While women rarely worked in the fields, many of them participated in the cleaning, sorting, and packing of fruit in packinghouses. (Huntington Library.)

This image shows the interior of a packinghouse in La Verne, California, in the early 20th century. Men and women working here washed, dried, and packed oranges and lemons for shipment by rail. By 1900, many citrus packinghouses had incorporated power-driven equipment to help sort fruit by sizes and wash it more effectively. (Wilson Library, University of La Verne.)

Claremont had numerous citrus packinghouses along the railroad tracks. This c. 1903 photograph of the Claremont Citrus Union packinghouse demonstrates how early orange packing relied extensively on human labor. Although new inventions improved productivity over time, the basic layout of packinghouses remained unchanged until the postwar years. Machines like mechanical washers and graders became common but never fully replaced human bodies. (Pomona Public Library.)

Just as photographers liked to showcase fieldworkers in the groves, they also preferred to line up packinghouse employees outside their workplace. The people shown here in 1906 worked at the packinghouse of the Pomona Fruit Growers Exchange. Like many packinghouses, this building was located on the tracks of a railroad—in this case, the Southern Pacific. (Pomona Public Library.)

Workers in the Redlands Golden Orange Association packinghouse may have resented being interrupted to pose for a photograph. Citrus crate labels, a common advertising mechanism used across the industry, are visible on some of the boxes on the periphery of this image. (A.K. Smiley Public Library.)

The interior of the Redlands Orange Growers packinghouse was typical of such structures in the citrus belt. Notable in this image, which was taken sometime between 1890 and 1910, are the packing crates used to ship oranges. The Rose Brand citrus crate label appears on the sides of these boxes. (A.K. Smiley Public Library.)

This undated photograph of the Redlands Orange Growers packinghouse highlights the role of electricity in modernizing the citrus industry in the 20th century. Electrical lighting and machines increased productivity, which extended the market for oranges and lemons from California. Machines even produced the citrus crates visible in the foreground and background. (A.K. Smiley Public Library.)

Citrus growers in California revamped packing through assembly lines. By 1910, electricity had revolutionized citrus packing, as shown in this 1910 image from Redlands. The workers in this packinghouse relied on power from Southern California Edison to place labels on orange crates, which connected citrus fruits sold across the country with California. (Huntington Library.)

Although female participation in the labor force dramatically expanded during World War II in the 1940s, women worked in California's citrus packinghouses decades before that. This image from Redlands was taken between 1890 and 1910 and includes women packing fruits into crates adorned with the Bronco Brand and Western American fruit labels used in that city. (A.K. Smiley Public Library.)

Fred Stebler (left) and George Parker (below) transformed packing in the citrus industry. Based in Riverside, Stebler's California Iron Works and Parker Machine Works designed and manufactured an assortment of devices for citrus packinghouses. These machines cleaned, sorted, and moved fruit through the assembly line. Parker and Stebler's feud drove innovations from both men. Eventually, their enterprises merged into the Stebler-Parker Company, which continued to supply devices that handled citrus fruits on their journey from packinghouses to refrigerator railroad cars. While both inventors worked in Riverside, members of the citrus industry across California purchased supplies from them. (Both, Museum of Riverside.)

MANUFACTURERS O

t Packers Machinery & Supplie

OFFICE

Workers at California Iron Works were subjected to photographs much like the workers in packinghouses. The widespread adoption of mechanized goods, including those produced by these workers, demonstrate how California's citrus agriculture played a key role in the state's industrial development. Like many of the packinghouses for which it provided manufactured goods, this building still stands, although it has been repurposed. (Museum of Riverside.)

The mechanization that transformed packinghouses significantly separated the California citrus industry from other forms of American agriculture, uniting farming with technological development. Innovations like this fruit elevator minimized the amount of human labor necessary to move oranges and lemons through packinghouses, demonstrating the benefits of motorization. (Museum of Riverside.)

Conveyor belts, a hallmark of assembly lines in the United States, became common in the citrus packinghouses of California thanks to the innovations of California Iron Works and Parker Machine Works. The conveyors produced by California Iron Works, which are shown in these images, used electrical power to move fruit. This allowed workers to complete other tasks, like packing fruit by hand or wheeling crates onto railcars. More than any other devices produced by George Parker or Fred Stebler, the conveyor belt epitomized the transformation of citrus packinghouses into technologically sophisticated industrial operations. (Both, Museum of Riverside.)

Among the most important tasks in a citrus packinghouse is the separation of oranges or lemons based on size and quality. Sizers—like the one from California Iron Works that is shown in this image—took this work out of the hands of human laborers and successfully automated it. (Museum of Riverside.)

Citrus growers in California prided themselves on the quality of their products. Packinghouse machines facilitated this through the standardization of washing and drying fruits. Mechanical fruit washers and cleaners, including the one shown here in 1926, helped to provide high-quality oranges and lemons to consumers across the United States. (Pomona Public Library.)

Mechanical Boxmaker.

Even an activity as simple as nailing an orange box had become mechanized by 1910. The two workers pictured in this packinghouse are manning a mechanical box-maker, which finished building the wooden crates used to ship oranges on railcars. (University of Southern California Libraries and California Historical Society.)

Industrial manufacturers provided an array of machines for citrus packers. This image shows a crate-nailing machine, which packers used to construct the wooden boxes used to transport oranges and lemons by rail. Relying on such devices improved productivity and profitability and solidified the mechanization of citrus agriculture. (Pomona Public Library.)

Inventors like Fred Stebler and George Parker continuously developed new methods to improve citrus packinghouses. The version of the orange-box maker shown here in the Covina Orange Growers Association packinghouse in 1943 was invented six years prior to this photograph's date of publication, well after packinghouses were first industrialized. The continued innovation of packinghouse machinery during the Great Depression attests to how well oranges and lemons sold even as a recession wracked the United States. (Claremont Colleges Libraries Special Collections.)

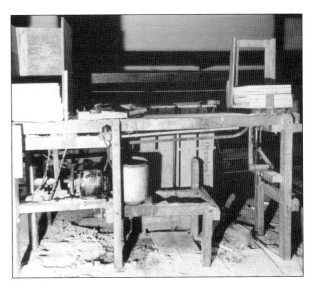

While many of Fred Stebler's machines handled oranges and lemons in bulk, the manufacturer constructed them to do so delicately to preserve the fruit's appearance. This fruit brusher from California Iron Works cleaned fruits as they wound along the conveyors of packinghouses—a key step in preserving the wholesome appearance of the Golden State's agricultural bounty. (Museum of Riverside.)

California citrus growers prided themselves on providing high-quality fruit to consumers. They selected only the finest lemons and oranges for shipment and prepared fruits using carefully maintained machinery, including this lemon washer pictured in Los Angeles around 1925. (University of Southern California Libraries and California Historical Society.)

Machines played important roles in branding the citrus bounty of the Golden State. This image features a printing machine stamping oranges with the name of the producer at the packinghouse of the Villa Park Orchards Association of Orange, California, in 1924, as a preternaturally serene employee guides the fruit. (Pomona Public Library.)

Among the more common but indispensable items furnished by California Iron Works was the clamp truck, shown here in action in a packinghouse. Workers relied on this device to quickly and easily move crates of oranges and lemons around packinghouses and onto railcars. (Museum of Riverside.)

Citrus growers measured how many oranges and lemons they sent from the Golden State to eastern markets by the carload. The tightly packed lemons visible in this car stopped at Los Angeles around 1925 suggests the immense volumes in which citrus growers dealt. (University of Southern California Libraries and California Historical Society.)

Packers fit as many fruits as possible into boxcars, such as the one pictured. The openings in the rear of the car stress the importance of proper ventilation in preventing lemons and oranges from spoiling in transit to markets. (A.K. Smiley Public Library.)

While California Iron Works and Parker Machine Works focused primarily on designing products for packinghouses, the companies' owners found time to patent devices that touched other aspects of the citrus industry. This ditchdigger from California Iron Works facilitated irrigation in citrus groves. (Museum of Riverside.)

Work in the citrus packinghouses was a multifaceted job, as shown in this photograph of the Upland Citrus Association around 1900. One crucial job was grading the fruit, which involved separating it by size and quality. Machines aided in this work, which was necessary in setting prices. (Huntington Library.)

Although white men owned most of the California citrus industry, every segment of society played a role in the commercial success of oranges and lemons. Women, notably from Hispanic backgrounds, made the California citrus industry thrive. While Mexican American men picked oranges in the field, women tended to work in the packinghouses. Despite the economic downturn of the Great Depression, citrus remained profitable thanks to women like these workers shown in a packinghouse in 1936. (Claremont Colleges Libraries Special Collections.)

Although it was not as closely connected with the citrus industry as its neighbors to the north, San Diego County did have orange and lemon groves. Fallbrook was a notable citrus center due in large part to packers like the women pictured here in 1949. (Los Angeles Times Photographic Archive [Collection 1429]. Library Special Collections, Charles E. Young Research Library, UCLA.)

Labor shortages during World War II led to opportunities for women to join the citrus industry. In addition to washing and grading fruit, female workers packed lemons and oranges before the fruits were loaded onto railroad cars. This photograph shows Francis Martinez (left) and Anita Ramirez (right) at the Foothill Packing House in Corona around 1946. (Corona Public Library.)

Women from various segments of society entered packinghouses to preserve California's citrus industry during and after World War II. Mexican American women became particularly prominent, including the ones shown here at the Duarte-Monrovia Fruit Exchange in 1947. (Los Angeles Times Photographic Archive [Collection 1429]. Library Special Collections, Charles E. Young Research Library, UCLA.)

By the 1940s, women had become indispensable to the citrus industry. The women shown here are packing lemons in Pomona, California, in 1940. As the decade continued and the United States entered World War II, with men joining the conflict against Japan and Germany, female laborers kept the citrus industry alive. (Pomona Public Library.)

The citrus industry would have failed without women like the workers from the Santa Ana–Tustin Citrus Association shown here in 1938. These women graded fruit based on size and appearance, separating higher quality specimens from culls that could be processed into byproducts. (Huntington Library.)

Women played major roles in the industrial processing of citrus fruits in California, as shown in this photograph of the College Heights Orange Association in Claremont. Note the gloves worn by these packers, which prevented the fruit from being scratched or damaged. (Pomona Public Library.)

Even substandard fruits could contribute to the financial success of citrus. For instance, poorer lemons could be repurposed into lemonade. The assembly line shown in a processing plant here in 1954 testifies to the enduring commercial importance of citrus, even as California's economy was shifting away from agriculture. (Huntington Library.)

Citrus packing became a fully industrialized activity in the 20th century, as demonstrated by buildings like the Santa Ana–Tustin Citrus Association in Orange County. This 1938 photograph suggests the scale of orange production in California. The wires at the top of the image draw attention to the electrification of packinghouses, which cemented the link between industry and agriculture in citrus production. (Huntington Library.)

Citrus from California was also sold abroad. The fruit grade checker shown here is inspecting lemons scheduled to be shipped from the Oxnard area to Great Britain in 1954. This was the first time fruits from the area had gone to England since World War II. (University of Southern California Libraries.)

Five

ADVERTISING AND CRATE LABELS

By the 1890s, California citrus growers had learned that they could thrive if they pooled their resources. In 1893, to overcome the challenges of fruit jobbers (wholesalers) in the distribution of oranges and lemons, citriculturists formed the Southern California Fruit Exchange. By 1905, this group had reorganized into the California Fruit Growers Exchange, perhaps better known by its brand name, Sunkist (for "sun-kissed," to cash in on the popularity of the Golden State's climate). By 1930, Sunkist controlled 75 percent of the oranges and almost all lemons grown in California.

With the rise of Sunkist, marketing and advertising became crucial to the citrus industry. The Southern Pacific and Santa Fe Railroads facilitated traveling exhibits, such as "California on Wheels," featuring California oranges and lemons alongside lectures and pamphlets that touted the benefits of citrus. In 1907, Sunkist partnered with the Southern Pacific Railroad for a promotional blitz targeting Iowa and the Midwest. The campaigns championed "Oranges for Health, California for Wealth."

Fairs were central to the promotion of the California citrus industry. In 1879, Eliza Tibbets's oranges won the top prizes at a citrus fair in Riverside. By 1884, at the world's fair in New Orleans, oranges from California edged out those grown in Florida to achieve first place. In 1886, the California Citrus Fair in Chicago enraptured the public. Most importantly, California citrus shone at the World's Columbian Exposition, a major fair held in Chicago in 1893 to commemorate the quadricentennial of Christopher Columbus's expeditions, garnering international attention.

Fairs and exhibitions persisted into the 20th century. Beginning in 1911, the city of San Bernardino hosted an annual National Orange Show to award a prize to the best orange. Not to be outdone, Orange County answered with its Valencia Orange Show at Anaheim in 1921, which ran for 10 years.

Images were key to Sunkist advertisements. Colorful crate labels placed on the sides of wooden boxes of fruits shipped to markets across the United States enticed buyers at eastern markets to purchase items grown in California, cementing brand loyalty in the process. Every orange and lemon packinghouse used these labels, and railroads carried them across the country.

By the 1880s, citrus from Southern California was appearing in world's fairs across the United States. These galas introduced potential consumers across the country and the world to oranges and lemons from the Golden State. This image shows Pomona's contribution to the world's fair of 1885. (Pomona Public Library.)

Photographs of citrus fairs extended the reach of promotional venues to larger audiences than those who attended in person. The 1890 State Citrus Fair in Pasadena, pictured here, showcased various fruits and byproducts that originated in the groves of Southern California. (Pomona Public Library.)

Early citrus fairs lacked the organizational finesse of later efforts but matched subsequent gatherings in scope. The Citrus State Fair of 1891, held in Los Angeles, featured some creative sculptures that exhibitors created with lemons and oranges. The citrus tower at the center of this image was replicated at the World's Columbian Exposition in Chicago in 1893. (Pomona Public Library.)

Charles C. Pierce took this photograph depicting the Duarte Exhibit of the Citrus Fair at Hazard Pavilion in Los Angeles in 1891. Orange sculptures, such as the tower featured here, were created at agricultural venues from the citrus belt to Chicago and Louisville, where exhibitions had touted fruits from California as early as the 1880s. (Huntington Library.)

This Ontario exhibit at the State Citrus Fair in 1891 fostered a sense of civic pride. The orange sculpture seen here was a recreation of the famous horse-drawn trolley that ran along Euclid Avenue, the main thoroughfare of Ontario. Horses pulled the car uphill, then rode down in the rear section of the vehicle. (A.K. Smiley Public Library.)

Redlands mounted an impressive display for the Southern California Citrus Fair of 1892. Although somewhat obscured, the words on the Redlands structure, visible near the rear of the image, read "Union Depot." This likely referred to the many railroad stations that serviced citrus country. (A.K. Smiley Public Library.)

The Tower of Oranges that graced the World's Columbian Exposition of 1893 enthralled visitors. This event, which was held in Chicago, Illinois, to commemorate the 400th anniversary of Christopher Columbus's first transhemispheric expedition, brought visitors from across the world to marvel at America's progress. Orange growers from the Golden State mounted this tower. (Claremont Colleges Libraries Special Collections.)

Expositions like the 1891 State Citrus Fair shown here touted the engineering accomplishments of citrus growers. The Redlands exhibit at that venue celebrated the Bear Valley Dam, which provided much-needed water from the San Bernardino Mountains to orange growers in inland Southern California. (A.K. Smiley Public Library.)

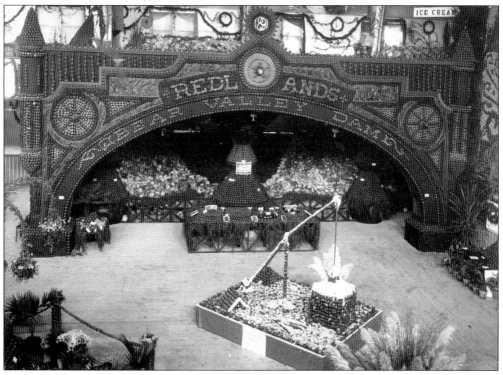

The citrus industry hired designers and lithographers to produce colorful images for labels to be placed on the sides of orange crates—a prototypical form of advertising. Early crate labels, like these Park Brand and Rose Brand images used in Redlands around 1900, pioneered design tactics that became definitive in later years. The use of oranges and lemons in tandem with flowers to frame groves combined photography with innovative graphic art. After the 1950s, when cardboard boxes replaced wooden crates, these labels became rare collectors' items. Early examples like these remain popular among aficionados of citrus history. (Both, A.K. Smiley Public Library.)

Citrus crate labels drew on patriotic imagery to link fruits with classic Americana. Uncle Sam proudly displays Washington navel oranges on this crate label that was used by a fruit company in Riverside. Through such images, oranges tied California to the United States as a whole. (Citrus Roots Collection.)

La Verne, the self-proclaimed "Heart of the Orange Empire," sat at the midpoint of the Pasadena-Riverside citrus belt. The image on this crate label from La Verne was meant to catch the attention of jobbers (wholesalers) at eastern markets and develop brand loyalty. Landscapes such as this one appeared on numerous labels. (Citrus Roots Collection.)

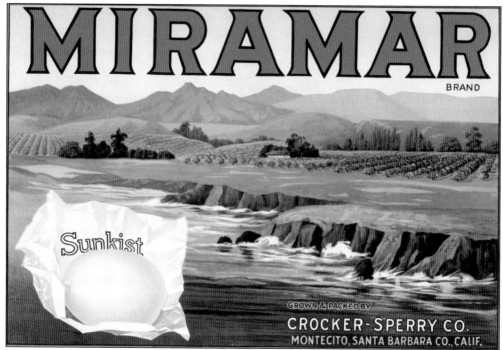

Images that rendered California as an earthly paradise saturated advertising by the 20th century, a trend to which the citrus industry wholeheartedly subscribed. The Pacific Ocean, a tantalizing feature that lured countless settlers to the American West, appeared on many citrus crate labels. Packinghouses in Santa Barbara and Ventura Counties frequently circulated vivid images such as these, which positioned orange and lemon groves directly on beachfronts. While trees typically did not appear directly adjacent to the ocean, some varieties of citrus, notably lemons, thrived on the warm coast from Santa Barbara to San Diego. (Both, Citrus Roots Collection.)

Portraying California as the linchpin that economically unites the United States, South America, and the Pacific Rim is not a 21st-century invention. Since the first transcontinental railroad crossed the United States, producers in California envisioned the region as the heart of a global trade network. Citrus growers shared that dream, as shown on this crate label. (Citrus Roots Collections.)

Western Lithograph Company, one of the leading producers of citrus crate labels, continued to print new images until cardboard boxes displaced wooden crates in the 1950s. This label from 1951 links lemons to California's coast, uniting two major features of advertising in the Golden State. Lemons did thrive in coastal areas like Ventura County, giving this label a ring of truth. (Huntington Library. Reprinted with permission of Ventura Pacific. All Rights Reserved.)

This citrus crate label brings together numerous common features of the genre. The image at the center fixes the viewer's eye on the lush valley, rolling hills, and purple mountains. While the label names the city where the lemons were produced (Goleta), it also relies on the more familiar name of Santa Barbara County to attract consumers. (Citrus Roots Collection, reprinted with permission of Sunkist Growers, Inc. and Ventura Pacific, Inc. All Rights Reserved.)

Riverside County generated impressive citrus crate labels. This image, originally printed in full color, drew attention to the city of Corona, which was famed for its lemon groves. The lemon depicted so vividly on this lithograph appeared far more brilliant than the fruits harvested in the groves, which had their distinctive yellow color revealed after they were cleaned at a packinghouse. (Citrus Roots Collection.)

Although the production of oranges and lemons outstripped that of other varieties of citrus in California, growers experimented with a variety of other strains. Grapefruit appeared in Riverside County in the early 20th century, as advertised on this crate label touting the virtues of those fruits grown in Coachella Valley. (Citrus Roots Collection.)

Beyond providing colorful graphics to attract jobbers, crate labels projected the civic pride of citriculturists. This c. 1900 label from Riverside draws attention the city's palm trees, spacious boulevards, and agricultural bounty. These had become common themes on citrus crate labels by the mid-20th century. (Huntington Library.)

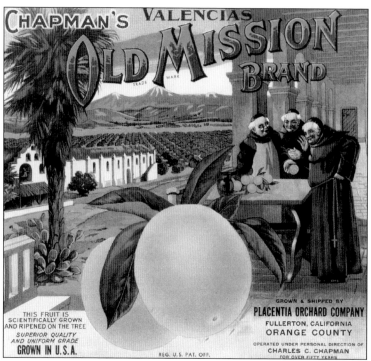

Crate labels like this one tapped into mission imagery and linked the citrus industry to the Spanish period of California history. Spanish friars did bring citrus fruits to the region, but Indigenous workers kept the trees alive. Charles C. Chapman, named on this label, was a pivotal figure in Orange County's citrus industry. (Citrus Roots Collection.)

Exhibitors at citrus fairs sometimes re-created citrus crate labels as exhibits, as shown in this transformation of Chapman's Old Orange Brand from a lithograph into a display at the Valencia Orange Show in 1921. (Los Angeles Times Photographic Archive [Collection 1429]. Library Special Collections, Charles E. Young Research Library, UCLA.)

The grounds of the National Orange Show in San Bernardino (pictured) became one of the most important sites in the promotion of the California citrus industry. Attendees at this event exchanged scientific methods for agriculture and competed for prizes. The architecture projects the Spanish Revival style common in Southern California in the early 20th century. (Pomona Public Library.)

In their quests for profits, promoters of the citrus industry commercialized minorities, women, and even the human body. In this image from the National Orange Show in San Bernardino in 1934, Irene Hatcher lent vivacity to Ontario's display. (Los Angeles Times Photographic Archive [Collection 1429]. Library Special Collections, Charles E. Young Research Library, UCLA.)

The National Orange Show in San Bernardino was the most important promotional venue for citrus production in the Golden State. Cities from across the citrus empire competed for the grand prize at this event. Pomona won top honors, receiving a blue ribbon and $300 for this display in 1931. (Pomona Public Library.)

San Diego County had lemon and orange groves as early as the 1880s. The county hosted several citrus fairs over the years and competed in the National Orange Show of San Diego; the Imperial County exhibit at that show is pictured here in 1954. (Pomona Public Library.)

Citrus fairs offered orange- and lemon-growing communities the opportunity to engage in friendly competition to see which places produced the best fruits. This image shows an exhibit built by the city of Pomona for the Riverside Orange Show in 1927. The photograph was taken by the studio of C.C. Brinkmen. (Pomona Public Library.)

By the 1920s, cities from across the California citrus belt were taking advantage of the National Orange Show in San Bernardino for the marketing attention it attracted. This overhead view from 1926 offers a sense of the scope of the event. (Los Angeles Times Photographic Archive [Collection 1429]. Library Special Collections, Charles E. Young Research Library, UCLA.)

In addition to awarding prices for fruits, citrus fairs crowned honorary monarchs. At the National Orange Show in San Bernardino in 1936, for example, Bernardine Voorhees was anointed queen. A re-creation of the state seal solidified the association between citrus agriculture and California's identity. (Los Angeles Times Photographic Archive [Collection 1429]. Library Special Collections, Charles E. Young Research Library, UCLA.)

Orange County also participated in the exhibition of citrus fruits. Starting in 1921, its Valencia Orange Show attracted vendors from across the citrus empire. An exhibit from the 1923 show is shown here. Note the citrus crate labels near the bottom of the photograph—these were used to create brand associations. (Pomona Public Library.)

This display created by the American Fruit Growers at the Valencia Orange Show in Anaheim demonstrates that city's deep connections to citrus. The Blue Goose pictured here also appeared on the labels of crates shipped by American Fruit Growers. Pres. Warren Harding opened this show when it was held in 1921. (Los Angeles Times Photographic Archive [Collection 1429]. Library Special Collections, Charles E. Young Research Library, UCLA.)

Towns in the citrus belt held parades to celebrate their agriculture. This 1933 Orange Parade in Riverside celebrated the 60th anniversary of the Washington navel orange industry. Note the tiered cake made from oranges that appears on the float. (Los Angeles Times Photographic Archive [Collection 1429]. Library Special Collections, Charles E. Young Research Library, UCLA.)

Scientific research in the 20th century provided new ways to promote the benefits of California's citrus bounty. Sunkist's 1920s advertisements frequently capitalized on these benefits. Under the direction of Don Francisco, the brilliant advertising manager of the California Fruit Growers Exchange, Sunkist ran advertisements touting the positive impact of vitamin C. Thanks to such advertisements, orange juice was ubiquitous on breakfast tables across the United States by the 1920s. Sunkist also drew attention to alternative uses for citrus, especially lemons, which took on a variety of roles, including in "Sunkist Lemon Pie." This full-color image targeted female consumers, who frequently made decisions regarding groceries. (Citrus Roots Collection, reprinted with permission of Sunkist Growers, Inc. All rights reserved.)

The California Fruit Growers Exchange (CFGE) revolutionized the marketing of oranges and lemons. Following a successful partnership with the Southern Pacific Railroad that involved advertising oranges east of the Rocky Mountains in 1907, the CFGE added advertising to its budget. Using its nationally renowned Sunkist brand, the CFGE employed an array of promotional strategies to build a national market for oranges and lemons. Advertisements appeared in periodicals across the country, as well as in railcars such as those of the Pacific Electric line that ran across Southern California. One successful strategy involved drawing attention to the health benefits of drinkable citrus commodities, namely orange juice and lemonade. This pair of advertisements from the 1920s stressed the positive impact of these beverages. (Citrus Roots Collection, reprinted with permission of Sunkist Growers, Inc. All rights reserved.)

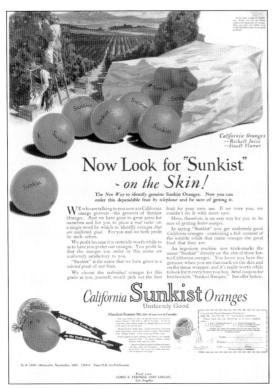

Sunkist's greatest accomplishment was the association of citrus fruits with its brand and California in the minds of consumers. Advertisements, fairs, and exhibits—as well as citrus crate labels—played important roles in the process, but not more than the actual fruits. As this advertisement pointed out, even the skin of an orange could be labeled "Sunkist." (Citrus Roots Collection, reprinted with permission of Sunkist Growers, Inc. All rights reserved.)

In addition to tapping into the language of "sun-kissed" California, Sunkist was far rosier than the organization's longer name, the California Fruit Growers Exchange. Promotional items and cookbooks, such as this recipe cover, offered creative suggestions for how to use oranges and lemons in the kitchen. (Citrus Roots Collection, reprinted with permission of Sunkist Growers, Inc. All rights reserved.)

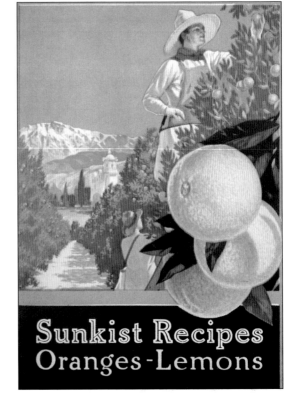

The citrus industry, often in cooperation with the railroads of Southern California, targeted consumers in midwestern states like Iowa, which is depicted here as a young boy accepting oranges from "Miss California." Orange growers flooded the state with fairs and lavish images to entice Iowans to buy fruits. (Citrus Roots Collection.)

To spread industry news, orange and lemon growers in the Golden State published their own periodical. The *California Citrograph* provided readers with information about updated agricultural methods, industrial developments, and profiles of successful figures within the citrus industry. This cover from a 1933 issue of the *California Citrograph* contrasts oranges with the gold rush, conflating two major aspects of the Golden State's history. (Citrus Roots Collection.)

Promoters of the citrus industry frequently tapped into the state's Spanish and Mexican heritage to advertise products. This San Diego exhibit at the National Orange Show in San Bernardino of 1953 was themed around Cinco de Mayo. However, the event commemorated by that holiday occurred after California became part of the United States. (Pomona Public Library.)

Every major citrus show crowned an orange queen. Donelia Dooley (pictured) received that honor at the National Orange Show in San Bernardino in March 1953. Dooley, a resident of nearby Highland, was only 17 at the time this photograph was taken. (Claremont Colleges Libraries Special Collections.)

Six

WATER, WEATHER, AND SCIENCE

Turning Southern California into an orange empire required citriculturists to reshape the landscape. The San Bernardino and San Gabriel Valleys, the heartland of the expanding orange empire, are semiarid, with only a handful of natural water sources. Although Spanish colonizers and Indigenous peoples working on the missions irrigated crops in the 18th century, by the 1890s, the scope of the orange and lemon groves that arose in the citrus heartland required more water. This resulted in large-scale water projects like the Bear Valley Dam in San Bernardino County or the Gage Canal that irrigated the groves of Riverside.

Additionally, the weather posed challenges to the orange empire. Devastating freezes such as those that occurred in 1913 and 1937 forced citrus growers to come up with a solution for cold orange and lemon trees. Devices such as air circulators became common. The most widely used inventions were orchard heaters, colloquially dubbed smudge pots because of the thick black vapor they discharged into the groves. Although smudge pots kept crops safe, they devastated the environment. Citrus growers also relied on broadcast communications, such as a radio program initiated by Floyd Young that informed growers of incoming cold fronts.

The relentless assault of insects and fungi led to revolutionary pest control methods across the citrus empire. Workers fumigated orange trees to exterminate bugs, but scientists also brought integrated pest management to the California citrus industry. When the cottony cushion scale menaced citrus groves at the end of the 19th century, entomologists from the US Department of Agriculture (USDA) enlisted Australian ladybugs to excise the pest. Later, under the leadership of G. Harold Powell, orange growers instructed field and packinghouse workers to handle fruit carefully to minimize the impact of fungal blue mold on the crops.

Efforts to control water, the weather, and pests led the California citrus industry to invest in scientific development. Following successful partnerships with railroads and the state government, leaders of the citrus industry successfully lobbied the University of California to start a Citrus Experiment Station in Riverside. Under the leadership of renowned botanist Herbert Webber, this station united leading scientists in efforts to scientifically safeguard citrus.

Early water projects in the citrus belt were simpler than the major efforts of the mid-20th century. This image shows wells used for the Gage Canal, which served Riverside, in approximately 1884. Named for émigré engineer Matthew Gage, the canal provided much-needed nourishment to the expanding Washington navel orange groves. As new groves appeared in Riverside, the Gage Canal expanded. (Citrus Roots Collection.)

Enormous water projects emerged to serve the orange empire as early as the 1880s. The Bear Valley Dam, completed in the San Bernardino Mountains in 1884, was one such venture. This impressive engineering feat was accompanied by what was the largest reservoir of water in California at the time. (Citrus Roots Collection.)

Citrus growers diverted large volumes of water from the few small rivers that run through Southern California. In San Bernardino, Riverside, and Orange Counties, the Santa Ana River served the needs of early agriculturalists. This image of a ditch on that body of water from the late 19th century demonstrates the simplicity of many early irrigation projects in the citrus belt. (Citrus Roots Collection.)

Irrigation channels, such as the one pictured here, brought water from the few rivers of Southern California to the plentiful orange and lemon fields. Before the need for water intensified in the 1910s and 1920s, simple stone flumes like this were sufficient to provide water to early citrus groves. (A.K. Smiley Public Library.)

Citrus trees require a steady supply of water, which is difficult to provide given the natural aridity of Southern California. Ditches and channels crisscrossed the groves of towns devoted to citriculture. This irrigated grove in Riverside is shown around 1895. (C.C. Pierce Photographic Collection [Collection 1756]. Library Special Collections, Charles E. Young Research Library, UCLA.)

Citriculturists used every available opportunity to trumpet their achievements in turning California into an empire of oranges and lemons. This hand-colored image originated in 1915 and was circulated at the Panama-California Exposition, which was held from 1915 to 1917 and invited guests from across the country to San Diego to commemorate the completion of the Panama Canal. (Pomona Public Library.)

When possible, citrus growers tapped into local sources of water, sinking wells into aquifers. Standpipes such as the one shown here were used for irrigation across the citrus empire. As groves became more common, these became insufficient, requiring growers to look elsewhere to meet their irrigation needs. (A.K. Smiley Public Library.)

While still technologically primitive by the standards of later endeavors, early fumigation in the California citrus industry was a large-scale effort. This image from 1893 shows a citrus grove being fumigated in Tustin and gives a sense of the enormous equipment required to lower canvas tents onto trees. (Pomona Public Library.)

To the promoters of California, every aspect of the citrus industry was ripe for advertising. This image depicting the fumigation of an orange grove was distributed at the Panama-Pacific International Exposition held in San Francisco in 1915. Adorning the top—or entire frame—with oranges became a recurring motif in promotional images associated with the citrus industry. (Pomona Public Library.)

Even early citrus agriculture in California relied on industrial development. This steam-drive spray rig used artificial power to augment human efforts in the orange empire as early as the 1890s. However, as indicated by the three-man crew, early machines were not efficient enough to entirely displace human labor. (Pomona Public Library.)

While new insects and plant diseases periodically afflicted orange and lemon groves, the adoption of new forms of technology transformed pest control in California's citrus empire. Packinghouses loyally patronized enterprises such as the Brogdex Company, which specialized in chemical fertilizers, pest control, and other agricultural technologies. Agents such as James Ward, whose pest control spray appears in use in Pomona, pioneered new ways to remove insects from trees. New technologies minimized safety hazards to workers, notably reducing the risk of chemical combustion that earlier fumigation tents often entailed. Despite these innovations, pests and diseases remain a problem in orange and lemon groves in the 21st century. (Both, Pomona Public Library.)

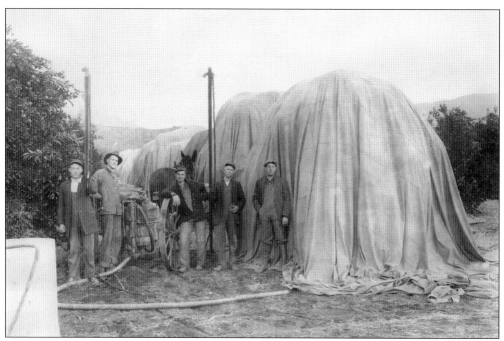

Working in the citrus industry frequently required laborers to operate industrial-strength pest control devices. This image shows a fumigation crew covering a tree in preparation of administering cyanide gas. Workers frequently fumigated orange and lemon trees at night to avoid causing photochemical reactions that could lead to fires. (Pomona Public Library.)

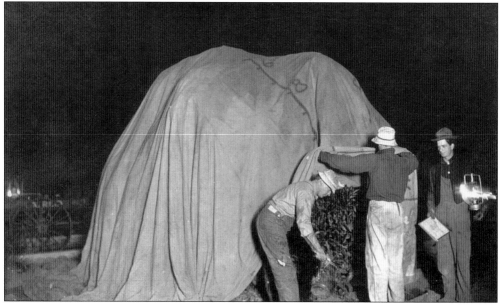

Fumigation was the most popular method for removing pests from California's citrus groves. Workers wrapped enormous bags around orange and lemon trees before fumigating them, as demonstrated in this picture taken near Pomona in 1906. Working in the groves at night required the use of artificial light, which was provided by lanterns in the early years of the citrus empire. (Pomona Public Library.)

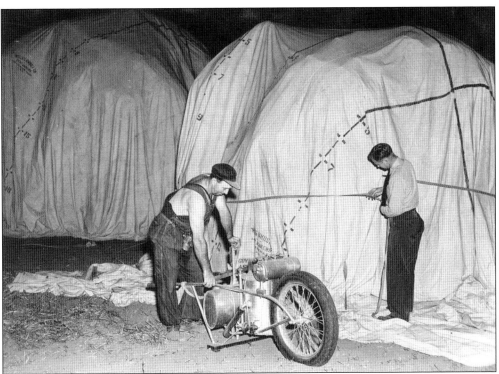

Unlike the simple farming of early US history, citriculture was a highly mechanized, scientifically managed enterprise. To protect oranges and lemons from a menagerie of insects, agricultural scientists in California developed special fumigants. Some fumigation methods required workers to tent trees, as shown above, while others involved simply spraying fruits, as pictured below. Both photographs were taken in 1938. Fumigation and scientific management curtailed the spread of a variety of pests and diseases, notably the cottony cushion scale and *tristeza*, or quick decline. Even the parent navel orange trees preserved in Riverside were infected by *Phytophthora gummosis*. One of the trees was saved by inarching (surgically grafting parts from healthy trees onto it). (Both, Los Angeles Agricultural Commissioner.)

Citrus growers could easily identify trees ravaged by pests, such as this specimen photographed around 1910. This leafy, blossoming tree—with its drooping branches brushing the ground—bears all the signs of infestation. Fumigating the tree could remove pests and potentially restore the plant. Fumigation required teams of workers; one pair of men operated the spray, while another two pulled the hoses, which extended 300 feet. (University of Southern California Libraries and California Historical Society.)

Although oranges accounted for more acreage than lemons in California, the latter variety of fruit received the same attention when it came to preventing pests and diseases. This c. 1938 image shows a lemon grove in the city of Riverside undergoing fumigation. (University of Southern California Libraries and California Historical Society.)

While early residents of the citrus empire praised California as a Mediterranean Eden, low temperatures could devastate oranges and lemons. A particularly frigid cold snap in 1913 killed many trees, including the unfortunate specimens captured in this image. The greatly diminished citrus crop of 1913 persuaded citriculturists to turn to scientific methods for managing the industry. (Pomona Public Library.)

The massive scope and impressive financial returns on citrus allowed agriculturalists to implement large-scale solutions to the problem of frost. This image of citrus trees on Magnolia Avenue in Riverside demonstrates the use of a latticed grove to prevent damage from frost around 1905. (Pomona Public Library.)

In addition to orchard heaters, citrus growers tested a variety of devices intended to prevent frost. The use of electrical power reduced the need for oil and coincided with California's push toward curbing emissions from heaters that could lead to smog. Windmills, such as the one shown here in 1954, were meant to increase circulation in the groves and help to prevent cool air from accumulating. (Pomona Public Library.)

Orchard heaters remained in use until the postwar period, when California finally mandated their removal. Earl Bosworth of Covina lit smudge pots in 1949, as shown here, to combat temperatures lower than 22 degrees Fahrenheit. Bosworth's oil can shows how workers poured oil into the devices and how smoke and flame emerged from the return stack. (Claremont Colleges Libraries Special Collections.)

Hauling oil to orchard heaters was no easy task, particularly in early groves and before the automobile became commonplace. This image shows a worker bringing a horse-drawn carriage with precious petroleum from the Union Oil Company of California into orange groves to prevent crops from freezing. (Pomona Public Library.)

Orchard heaters burned primarily during the evening, as shown in this image of an orange grove in Southern California. The devices were referred to as smudge pots due to the thick vapor they produced. While they helped growers blunt the impact of frost on orange and lemons, they had a detrimental impact on the environment. (Pomona Public Library.)

Relying on oil to fuel orchard heaters could be fatal to citrus trees. This 1914 image of a grove in Corona captures the aftermath of an oil spill. In addition to cracking the curb, the spill damaged a few trees. Despite causing frequent property damage and posing a danger to workers, orchard heaters remained in use until after World War II. (Pomona Public Library.)

The smoke produced by orchard heaters coalesced into enormous clouds of thick black vapor. This photograph depicts the city of Pomona at approximately 9:00 a.m. At one point in 1922, orchard heaters produced so much smog that it was carried to the coast and choked out the lighthouses at Los Angeles Harbor. (Pomona Public Library.)

Although snow was highly uncommon in the region, it did occasionally afflict the citrus industry in Southern California. Not even the orchard heaters, pictured here under a thick winter blanket, could save fruits from the caprices of nature, particularly when the return stacks were clogged with snow. (A.K. Smiley Public Library.)

Telecommunication played a vital role in citrus growers' efforts to control frost. Broadcaster Floyd Young, shown here in 1955, inaugurated a Fruit-Frost Protection Service that warned subscribers by phone of incoming inclement weather. By 1930, Young had partnered with radio station KNX to broadcast weather reports from the citrus town of Pomona. (Pomona Public Library.)

Technical development safeguarded fruits in transit from California to markets across the United States. Scientist G. Harold Powell (second from left), pictured here around 1905, promoted the careful handling of fruit, a method that stressed the need for workers to not bruise or damage the skin of oranges and lemons. Powell's "careful handling" ideology led to the reduction of blue mold, a pestilence that afflicted oranges around 1900. (Citrus Roots Collection.)

Running electrical wires through citrus groves afforded new possibilities for the prevention of frost. New but simple technologies included therapeutic lamps, such as the ones shown here being installed by Quentin Bashore in Covina in 1939. (Los Angeles Times Photographic Archive [Collection 1429]. Library Special Collections, Charles E. Young Research Library, UCLA.)

Icing and cooling stations across Southern California played a crucial role in preparing crops for the long journey by rail across the hot, arid American West. Cooling plants, such as the one shown here in Claremont, produced ice that prevented oranges and lemons from spoiling. (Claremont Colleges Libraries Special Collections.)

Railroads played key roles in the preservation of fruits from California during transit. The Southern Pacific and Santa Fe Railroads opened icing plants across the state, from Roseville to Colton. Ventilated and refrigerated railroad cars kept oranges and lemons from freezing. This photograph shows a worker preparing to load ice onto a refrigerator car. (Citrus Roots Collection.)

The Citrus Experiment Station, which opened in 1907 in Riverside as part of the University of California, brought together botanists, entomologists, and other scientists with the single goal of supporting the production of oranges and lemons. The station provided scientific and technological breakthroughs and spread information to growers about its discoveries through lectures and publications. (UC Riverside.)

Many important scientific tests and technical innovations occurred at the Citrus Experiment Station, shown here in 1925. The station was intended to promote scientific farming and address problems such as pest control and inclement weather. It laid the groundwork for the opening of a full campus of the University of California in Riverside in 1954. (Pomona Public Library.)

The Citrus Experiment Station in Riverside united nationally renowned experts with the single purpose of protecting trees, which thereby secured profitability. Scientists at the station devised numerous methods for improving the cultivation of oranges and lemons. This extended to various means of delivering water to groves. The photograph at right, taken during the summer of 1939, shows a plot of land that had been fertilized with ammonium sulfate and was using basin irrigation for water. The below image centers on a citrus tree in a tub next to a trough in 1934. (Both, Harry French Blaney Papers [Collection 1682]. Library Special Collections, Charles E. Young Research Library, UCLA.)

Even beyond the Citrus Experiment Station, orange and lemon growers employed scientists to come up with new uses for their fruits. These experts devised countless products that allowed growers to utilize low-quality fruits that otherwise could not have been sold. Byproducts included orange juice, which Sunkist turned into a staple of the American breakfast. The man in the above image is filling containers with oil of lemon in Corona, California, around 1925. In the below image, a chemist uses a polariscope to examine lemon oil in Corona around 1930. (Both, University of Southern California Libraries and California Historical Society.)

Seven

FALL OF THE EMPIRE

Against all commercial odds, the citrus industry performed unexpectedly well during the Great Depression of the 1930s. Consumption never flagged during that economically troubled decade, while production and the prices of oranges rose across the United States. However, industrial development in the following decade spelled change for the orange empire.

Following the explosive growth of factories in Southern California in the 1940s, primarily to produce aircraft and other wartime goods during World War II, a rapid influx of soldiers, sailors, and industrial workers flowed into the southland. As the defense industry and its auxiliary economic sectors boomed, urban and suburban development expanded, particularly in the form of tract housing.

The proliferation of houses caused orange and lemon groves to recede in the postwar decades. By the 1950s, a comprehensive network of highways, funded by the state and federal government, crisscrossed Southern California, necessitating the removal of citrus groves. In Anaheim, for instance, Valencia orange trees were removed to make way for Interstate 5, the Golden State Freeway, and filmmaker Walt Disney's amusement park, Disneyland.

While citrus acreage plummeted across the Southland, the orange empire migrated north and expanded. By the late 20th century, the Central Valley had become the new heartland of citrus agriculture in California. From 1950 to 2000, orange agriculture recovered dramatically as it recentered in the Central Valley. By 2007, California was producing 80 percent of America's table oranges and 90 percent of its lemons. This prodigious volume generated over $1 billion for growers annually. Mexican American laborers remained the indispensable backbone of the agricultural labor force—a position they had held since before the Great Depression. Some small plantings remain in some corners of the southland, such as lemon groves in Goleta and the Citrus State Historic Park in Riverside.

Sunkist Growers, Inc., descended from the California Fruit Growers Exchange (founded in 1893), remains a vital force within the citrus industry. It relocated from its headquarters in Los Angeles to the appropriately named Valencia in 2014, bringing the organization closer to the Central Valley. Sunkist continues to produce and ship oranges across the United States. For all the changes that have reshaped the orange and lemon groves of California since the 1940s, Sunkist's role remains essential, providing the citrus industry with an important connection to history.

The years immediately after the end of World War II represented a high point for citrus in Southern California. Packinghouses sometimes became the sites for field trips, as shown here in 1953, when students from the Claremont Colleges visited a packinghouse in Los Angeles. The image conveys how advanced the machinery in packinghouses had become in the postwar period as the citrus industry started to decline. (Los Angeles Daily News Negatives [Collection 1387]. Library Special Collections, Charles E. Young Research Library, UCLA.)

By the 1950s, California was beginning to reconfigure its infrastructure around automobile travel. As a result, developers uprooted citrus groves across the southern part of the state to make space for highways. This 1957 photograph of the Santa Ana Freeway (State Highway 57) shows how the postwar proliferation of houses—and the robust highway system that serviced the residents of those homes—displaced orange and lemon groves. Even Disneyland, Walt Disney's famed theme park, was built on an uprooted Valencia orange grove. (Citrus Roots Collection.)

Orange County truly lived up to its name in the postwar years. Thoroughfares such as Golden Avenue, Placentia, pictured here in 1961, attested to the continuation of citrus agriculture even as industrial development and housing displaced groves. Enhanced images like this color photograph offered even more vivid glimpses of the citrus industry than those of previous decades. (Citrus Roots Collection.)

The California Fruit Growers Exchange and its Sunkist brand represented the majority of citrus producers in California, but other cooperatives joined it in the first decades of the 20th century. Mutual Orange Distributors, formed in Redlands in 1906, became the second-largest citrus cooperative in the Golden State. (A.K. Smiley Public Library.)

Following the decline of railroads as the dominant form of shipping crops in the postwar era, growers exported citrus fruits from California in other ways. This photograph of Long Beach Harbor in 1975 shows a worker loading lemons onto a boat for international shipment. (Los Angeles Times Photographic Archive [Collection 1429]. Library Special Collections, Charles E. Young Research Library, UCLA.)

Leaders of the citrus industry cherished California's long-standing reputation for top-notch oranges and lemons. They convinced the state government to prevent outside fruits from entering California and potentially introducing pests. In this image, workers with the California Department of Transportation are erecting a sign along the Long Beach Freeway to warn against Mexican fruit flies, which pestered citrus trees. (Los Angeles Times Photographic Archive [Collection 1429]. Library Special Collections, Charles E. Young Research Library, UCLA.)

Following World War II and the rapid urbanization of the southland, the bulk of citrus production in California shifted to the Central Valley—primarily its southern portion, the San Joaquin Valley. There, a wide variety of citrus fruits thrive, including the mandarin oranges pictured here around 2014. (*Citrograph Magazine*.)

The citrus industry remains at the forefront of scientific and technological development. Electrostatic sprayers, such as the one shown here in 2014, deploy safer chemicals than those used in the early groves of the 1890s. More importantly, they offer the added benefit of not endangering fieldworkers. (*Citrograph Magazine*).

The Gage Canal continues to flow and now winds through the California Citrus State Historic Park at Riverside, which is pictured in 2015. This state park preserves a wide variety of citrus strains, including the vaunted Washington navel orange that catapulted Riverside to commercial success in the 19th century. (Photograph by the author.)

Even the contemporary citrus industry is not immune to the march of technological progress. Some scientists have pioneered the use of drones, such as this one shown in a nursery in Oregon monitoring crops. This image was published in *Citrograph Magazine* by the California Citrus Research Board. Drones have also been used to monitor the health of citrus trees in the Golden State. (*Citrograph Magazine*.)

Although pest management and chemical treatments remain effective tools, diseases and insects continue to target the citrus industry. Among the most notorious enemies of orange and lemon trees in California are the Asian citrus psyllid and huanglongbing (HLB). The trees in this grove, which was infested by HLB around 2016, developed heavy fruits. (*Citrograph Magazine*.)

Citrus growers in California continue to cooperate to maximize their industry's profitability. Sunkist Growers, Inc., remains a vital force in California citrus, as do trade shows and exhibitions, where producers exchange information on techniques and scientific developments. The 2016 Citrus Showcase at Visalia pictured here included this demonstration of a fruit wash designed by Fruit Growers Supply. (*Citrograph Magazine*.)

Public and private agencies remain committed to the success of the California citrus industry. These include the Citrus Research Board and the California Department of Agriculture. Among the most important entities fighting to preserve orange trees are the California Citrus Disease and Prevention Program; the group's representative David Morgan is pictured in 2017 in Bakersfield, where he was educating members of the media about citrus diseases. (*Citrograph Magazine.*)

One of the most important botanical archives dedicated to the citrus industry remains in Southern California. At Riverside, the University of California's Citrus Variety Collection continues the work started by the Citrus Experiment Station over a century ago. Strains of hybrid fruits—such as the limequats shown here, which are part of the Citrus Clonal Protection Program—thrive in Riverside. (*Citrograph Magazine.*)

BIBLIOGRAPHY

Farmer, Jared. *Trees in Paradise: A California History*. New York: W.W. Norton & Company, 2013.

Jenkins, Benjamin T. "The Octopus's Garden: Railroads, Citrus Agriculture, and the Emergence of Southern California." PhD dissertation, University of California, Riverside, 2016.

Klotz, Esther, Harry Lawton, and Joan H. Hall, eds. *A History of Citrus in the Riverside Area*, rev. ed. Riverside, CA: Riverside Museum Press, 1989.

Laszlo, Pierre. *Citrus: A History*. Chicago: University of Chicago Press, 2008.

Moses, H. Vincent. "The Flying Wedge of Cooperation: G. Harold Powell, California Orange Growers, and the Corporate Reconstruction of American Agriculture, 1904–1922." PhD dissertation, University of California, Riverside, 1994.

Ortlieb, Patricia, and Peter Economy. *Creating an Orange Utopia: Eliza Lovell Tibbets and the Birth of California's Citrus Industry*. West Chester, PA: Swedenborg Foundation Press, 2011.

Sackman, Douglas Cazaux. *Orange Empire: California and the Fruits of Eden*. Berkeley: University of California Press, 2005.

Sunkist. "Sunkist Growers Moves Headquarters to Valencia." Sunkist.com, August 12, 2014. https://www.sunkist.com/press-room/sunkist-move.

Tobey, Ronald, Charles Wetherell, Kevin Hallaran, and Buffie Hollis. *The National Orange Company Packing House: An Architectural and Technological History, 1898–1940*. Riverside: Laboratory for Historical Research, Department of History, University of California, Riverside, 1991.

DISCOVER THOUSANDS OF LOCAL HISTORY BOOKS FEATURING MILLIONS OF VINTAGE IMAGES

Arcadia Publishing, the leading local history publisher in the United States, is committed to making history accessible and meaningful through publishing books that celebrate and preserve the heritage of America's people and places.

Find more books like this at
www.arcadiapublishing.com

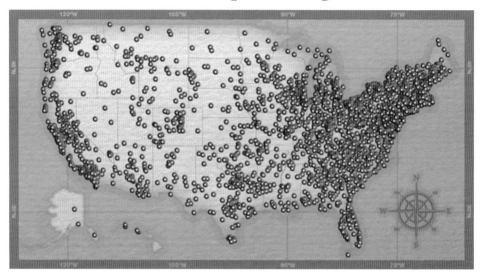

Search for your hometown history, your old stomping grounds, and even your favorite sports team.

Consistent with our mission to preserve history on a local level, this book was printed in South Carolina on American-made paper and manufactured entirely in the United States. Products carrying the accredited Forest Stewardship Council (FSC) label are printed on 100 percent FSC-certified paper.

MADE IN THE USA